apple

WATERFORD TOWNSHIP
PUBLIC LIBRARY

P9-ELX-494

J 745.594 MCG

5559

Paper crafts for Chinese New
Year
McGee, Randel
J 745.594 MCG

DISCARD

# Paper Crafts for Chinese New Year

Randel McGee

**Enslow Elementary**

an imprint of

**Enslow Publishers, Inc.**

40 Industrial Road
Box 398
Berkeley Heights, NJ 07922
USA

http://www.enslow.com

*For my favorite (and only) daughter, Melanie Ann!*
*She is a great artist, teacher, and inspiration!*

This book meets the National Standards for Arts Education standards.

Enslow Elementary, an imprint of Enslow Publishers, Inc.

Enslow Elementary® is a registered trademark of Enslow Publishers, Inc.

Copyright © 2008 by Enslow Publishers, Inc.

All rights reserved.

No part of this book may be reproduced by any means
without the written permission of the publisher.

**Library of Congress Cataloging-in-Publication Data**

McGee, Randel.
    Paper crafts for Chinese New Year / Randel McGee.
        p. cm. — (Paper craft fun for holidays)
    Summary: "Explains the significance of Chinese New Year and how to make crafts out of paper"—
        Provided by publisher.
    Includes bibliographical references and index.
    ISBN-13: 978-0-7660-2950-7
    ISBN-10: 0-7660-2950-6
    1. Holiday decorations—Juvenile literature. 2. Paper work—Juvenile literature. 3. Chinese New Year—
        Juvenile literature. I. Title.
    TT900.H6M33 2008
    745.594'1—dc22

                                        2007014026

Printed in the United States of America

10 9 8 7 6 5 4 3 2

**To Our Readers:**
We have done our best to make sure all Internet Addresses in this book were active and appropriate when we went to press. However, the author and the publisher have no control over and assume no liability for the material available on those Internet sites or on other Web sites they may link to. Any comments or suggestions can be sent by e-mail to comments@enslow.com or to the address on the back cover.

Every effort has been made to locate all copyright holders of material used in this book. If any errors or omissions have occurred, corrections will be made in future editions of this book.

**Illustration Credits:** Crafts prepared by Randel McGee; photography by Nicole diMella/Enslow Publishers, Inc.; Shutterstock, pp. 4, 5, 45.

**Cover Illustration:** Crafts prepared by Randel McGee; photography by Nicole diMella/Enslow Publishers, Inc.

# CONTENTS

# Chinese New Year!

It is late January or early February. The streets of a large city are bustling with people. Suddenly a large, colorful dragon dances in the street! Drums and gongs sound everywhere. Firecrackers explode all around! Fireworks light up the night! People shout "Gung hay fat choy!" and "Happy New Year!" These people are celebrating the Chinese New Year following a calendar that is much older than the calendar we use today.

Chinese history says that the lunar calendar and method for counting days, weeks, and years was invented by Emperor Huang Ti about 2637 B.C.E. The emperor's calendar was based on a scientific study of the cycles of the sun and moon.

The Chinese still use their lunar calendar to set dates for traditional celebrations. The Chinese New Year begins with the second new moon (the dark phase of the moon) after the winter solstice (the shortest day of the year) and ends with the next full moon fifteen days later. Each year is named for one of twelve animals in the Chinese zodiac, or star cycle.

The Chinese have many fun and lively traditions celebrating the first fifteen days of the New Year. On the first day, they welcome all the gods of heaven and do not eat meat. The second day, they pray to their ancestors and are extra kind to their pet dogs, as this is the day to honor all dogs. On the third and fourth days, all married men are supposed to pay special honor to their parents-in-law. On day five, everyone stays home to welcome the "God of Wealth." It is bad luck to visit friends on this day. From the sixth to the tenth day they will visit their friends and relatives. The seventh day is considered everyone's birthday and eating noodles on this day means you will have a long life. The tenth through twelfth days are to invite relatives for dinner. The thirteenth is a day of simple foods, after all the big dinners of the previous three days. The

fourteenth day is to get ready for the last day of celebration. The fifteenth day is the Lantern Festival when children carry lanterns around their neighborhoods at night as they visit their friends.

The Dragon Parade and the Lion Dance are important parts of this celebration. The dragon is said to bring good fortune and the lion scares evil away. During the fifteen days of the New Year celebration Chinese decorate their homes with the symbols for luck, fortune, happiness, and prosperity in hope that these good things will stay in their homes throughout the year.

# DANCING DRAGON PUPPET

During the Chinese New Year celebration a large, colorful dragon dances in the streets. The dragon costume is made with a big papier-mâché head and a long cloth body with many people inside to make it dance and slither along. It is thought that the longer the body is, the more good luck will come to the village. The movements are slithery like a snake, with the dragon's head looking from side to side and dipping up and down. The dragons are often brightly colored in red (considered a lucky color in China), green, or gold. Make your own miniature dragon puppet.

## WHAT YOU WILL NEED

- ✎ 2 toilet tissue tubes
- ✎ scissors
- ✎ poster paint
- ✎ paintbrush
- ✎ crepe-paper streamers in any color
- ✎ white glue
- ✎ construction paper in any color
- ✎ clear tape
- ✎ 2 chopsticks or 10-inch-long thin dowels

# WHAT TO DO

**A)**

1. Cut two small triangles across from each other on one end of one of the toilet tissue tubes. This tube will form the dragon's head (See A). Cut the other tube at an angle. This will be the dragon's tail.

2. Paint the outside of the tubes as you wish with poster paint. Let dry.

**B)**

3. Cut four 10-inch-long pieces of crepe-paper streamers. The pieces can be any color you like. Glue the long edges of the pieces together to form one wide sheet of crepe paper (See B). Let dry.

WATERFORD TOWNSHIP PUBLIC LIBRARY

100623

C)

**4.** Cut different shapes from construction paper to add eyes, teeth, horns, whiskers, and scales to your dragon's head and tail (See C).

**5.** Tape one short side of the sheet of crepe paper to the back edge of the head. Tape the other end of the crepe paper to the uncut end of the tail piece.

**6.** On the underside of the head and tail, ask an adult to help poke a hole in the middle of each one using scissors.

**7.** Push a chopstick or dowel up through the hole. Tape it in place inside the tube. Do the same with the second chopstick and second hole (See D).

D)

# TANGRAM

This is a puzzle and creative game from China. It is not known how old it is, but the first book about it appeared in China in 1813. It is popular throughout China and is a fun game to play when visiting friends and relatives during the sixth through tenth days of the New Year celebration.

The rules are simple: Use all the shapes, or tans, from the puzzle; make sure they all touch another piece, but do not let them overlap; create a recognizable design. Use your imagination!

## WHAT YOU WILL NEED

- ✎ pencil
- ✎ ruler
- ✎ construction paper in any color
- ✎ scissors
- ✎ office paper in any color
- ✎ white glue

# WHAT TO DO

1. Draw a 4-inch x 4-inch square on a piece of construction paper. Use a ruler to make seven different shapes in the square (See A). (See page 38 for the pattern).

2. Cut out the square and the shapes inside the square.

A)

**B)**

3. Arrange the tan into interesting shapes and designs on a sheet of office paper (See B).

4. When you have a design you like, glue it in place. Let dry.

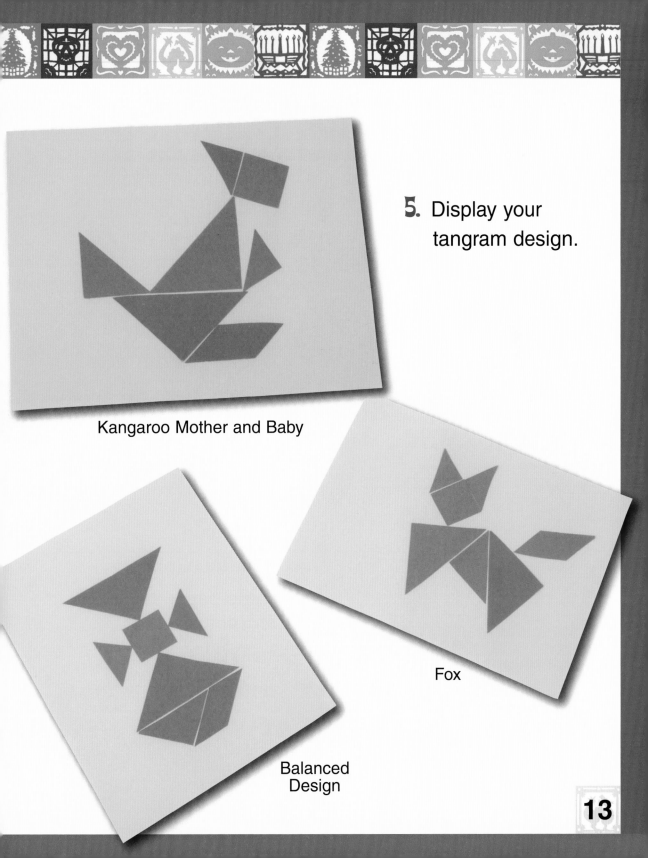

Kangaroo Mother and Baby

**5.** Display your tangram design.

Fox

Balanced
Design

# LION DANCER MASK

In China, a dancing lion is thought to scare away evil and welcome happiness. The Chinese people have been performing lion dances since about 300 B.C.E. During the fourth through fifteenth day of the New Year, two-man teams will visit different villages to perform a lively lion dance and bring good luck to the village. You can wear your lion mask during your Chinese New Year celebration.

## WHAT YOU WILL NEED

- white card stock
- tracing paper
- pencil
- scissors
- crayons or markers
- construction paper in any color (optional)

- white glue
- clear tape (optional)
- crepe-paper streamers in any color
- masking tape
- yarn

# WHAT TO DO

**1.** Fold your card stock in half width-wise so that it looks like a book.

**2.** Use tracing paper to transfer the pattern from page 38 to the folded card stock. Put the flat edge of the pattern along the fold.

A)

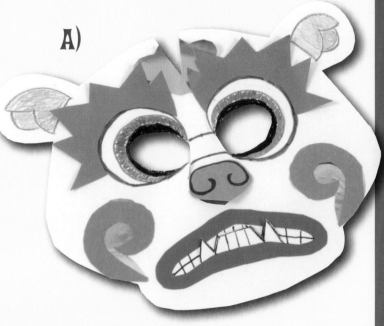

**3.** Cut out the solid lines of the pattern.

**4.** Open the mask and decorate it with crayons, markers, colored paper shapes, or anything else you wish (See A).

**B)**

**5.** Glue eight or ten 4-inch-long crepe-paper streamers (See B) around the edge of the mask. Let dry. Cut along the crepe paper streamer to form more strands of hair.

**C)**

**6.** Fold along the dotted lines indicated on the pattern (See C). On page 38 there is an explanation of how to fold the dotted lines.

7. Overlap the flaps at the top of the mask about a half-inch. Glue or tape them together. Let dry.

8. Cut two 12-inch pieces of yarn. On the back of the mask, tape a piece of yarn on each side near the eye openings to tie comfortably around your head (See D).

D)

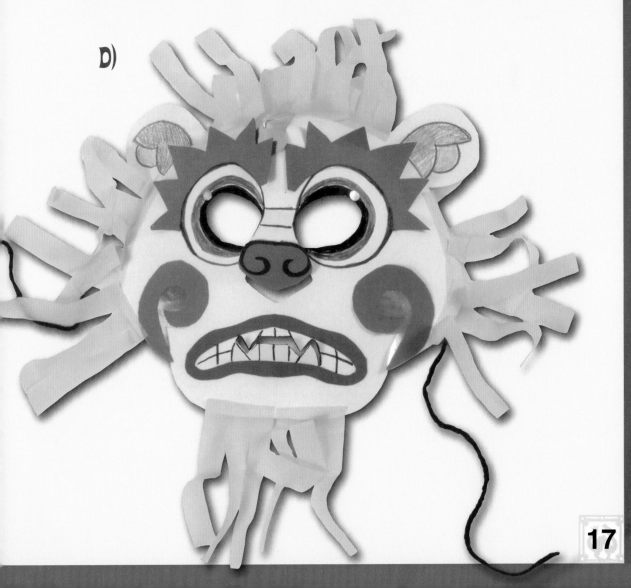

# LAI SEE, RED GIFT ENVELOPE

The Chinese believe that bright red is a color that attracts energy, good luck, and success with money. A New Year greeting or gift in a red envelope, called *lai see*, is especially lucky. When children and young, unmarried adults go visiting during the New Year celebration, they will often receive *lai see*. It will hold a greeting card or gift of money inside. Make your own *lai see*, and a greeting card to give to your friends and relatives for the New Year.

## WHAT YOU WILL NEED

- tracing paper
- pencil
- red office paper
- scissors
- white glue
- gold glitter glue (optional)
- gold foil wrapping paper (optional)
- index cards, 4 inches x 6 inches, in any color
- clear tape (optional)

# WHAT TO DO

1. Use tracing paper and a pencil to trace the envelope pattern on page 40.

A)

2. Transfer the envelope pattern to the red office paper (See A). Cut out the pattern.

**B)**

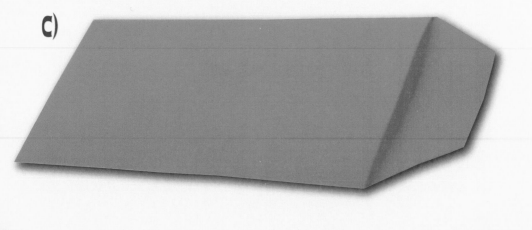

**3.** Fold the envelope along the fold lines as indicated on the pattern (See B). Glue the edge and bottom flap to form a long envelope (See C). Let dry.

**C)**

**4.** Decorate the envelope with glue and glitter, or gold foil as you wish (See D). Let dry. See page 42–43 for the Chinese symbols.

**5.** Write a New Year greeting on the index card and decorate it as you wish. Some examples are shown. Let dry. Put it in your *lai see*.

**6.** Fold the top flap and seal the *lai see* with a small piece of clear tape.

D)

E)

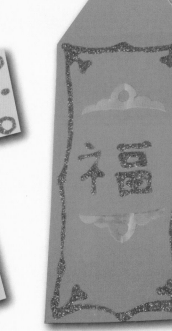

Best Wishes for a Happy Year!

I hope you have a Happy New Year!

Melanie, Lots of Success in the New Year! Nathan

May you have Happiness in the New Year!

# SHADOW PUPPETS

Some scholars believe that the Chinese developed the art of shadow puppetry at least one thousand years ago. Today there are many troupes, or performing groups, of shadow puppeteers throughout China. The puppets are traditionally cut from thin, stiff leather and are flat. They are usually designed in profile (seen from the side). The puppets are placed against a cloth screen, and a bright light is shown from behind the puppets. The audience on the other side of the screen sees the shadows of the puppets. Folktales are told using shadow puppets. You can share a shadow puppet story with your family and friends.

## WHAT YOU WILL NEED

- ✎ pencil
- ✎ poster board or light cardboard
- ✎ crayons or markers
- ✎ scissors
- ✎ masking tape
- ✎ an unsharpened pencil or chopstick
- ✎ white wrapping paper or butcher paper
- ✎ small reading lamp

# WHAT TO DO

1. Draw a puppet character on the poster board. See page 41 for the patterns. Decorate the puppets as you wish using crayons or markers.

2. Cut out the puppets.

**A)**

**3.** Cut two 2-inch-long pieces of masking tape and place them at the tip of the unsharpened pencil or chopstick so that it forms a T-shape.

**4.** Fasten the loose ends of the masking tape to the back of the puppet (See A).

5. With an adult's help, tape a piece of white wrapping paper or butcher paper across a doorway.

6. Use a small reading lamp to light the white wrapping paper. Put on a puppet show for your family and friends.

# CHINESE LANTERN

The fifteenth night, the last night, of the Chinese New Year is the Lantern Festival. On this night, communities have special displays of beautiful lanterns in all shapes and sizes. Children stroll through their neighborhoods and visit their friends carrying little lanterns. The lantern is a symbol of hope and celebration. Lanterns are often decorated with pictures of flowers, lions, or dragons.

## WHAT YOU WILL NEED

- ✎ red construction paper, 12 inches x 18 inches
- ✎ tracing paper
- ✎ pencil
- ✎ scissors
- ✎ ruler
- ✎ crayons or markers
- ✎ white glue
- ✎ clear tape
- ✎ yarn

# WHAT TO DO

A)

1. Fold the red construction paper in half width wise so that it looks like a book. Fold the paper in half again (See A).

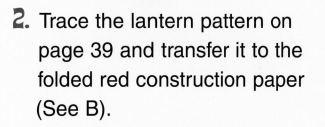

2. Trace the lantern pattern on page 39 and transfer it to the folded red construction paper (See B).

B)

3. Cut out the pattern. Be sure to cut through all layers of the folded red paper.

**4.** Cut four pieces of tracing paper 4 inches x 6 inches. Decorate these four pieces with crayons or markers. Let dry.

**5.** Open the cut out red paper and lay it in front of you. Tape or glue the decorated tracing paper pieces over the openings in the lantern pattern (See C).

C)

**6.** Tape the two edges of the lantern together.

**7.** Gently pinch each fold of the lantern so that it forms four even corners.

**8.** Cut a 12-inch piece of yarn. Tape the ends of the yarn to opposite sides of the top of the lantern to hold it or to hang it (See D). Have an adult help you hang the lantern.

D)

# FIRECRACKER DECORATIONS

In Chinese legends, Nian is a monster that waits to eat people during the New Year celebrations. He was so large that he could swallow several people in one gulp! A wise old man was able to find the monster, train him to be ridden, and learn of his secret fears. Before the old man rode away on the fierce beast, he told the people that Nian was afraid of the color red, bright lights, and loud noises.

## WHAT YOU WILL NEED

- toilet tissue tube
- white glue
- paintbrush
- red tissue paper
- scissors
- yarn
- yellow tissue paper

The Chinese make strings of firecrackers wrapped in red tissue paper and light them to make sure that Nian does not return. This firecracker decoration does not explode or make noise, but it will work just as well to scare any monsters from your celebration.

# WHAT TO DO

1. Coat the toilet tissue tube lightly with glue.

**A)**

2. Carefully wrap the red tissue paper around the tube (See A). Leave about an inch of tissue paper sticking over both ends of the tube. Glue the edges and let them dry.

3. Twist the extra tissue at one end of the tube and tuck it inside the tube.

**4.** Cut a 5-inch piece of yarn. At the other end of the tube, place the yarn into the tube with some of the yarn sticking out of the tissue paper (See B). Twist the tissue paper around the yarn. This is the fuse. Put a dot of glue where the yarn and tissue paper meet. Let dry.

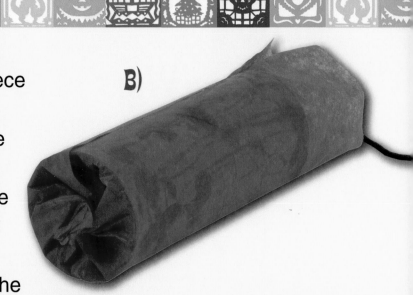

B)

**5.** Cut a zigzagged line across the center of the tube, but do not cut all the way through. Gently bend the tube to open at the zigzagged line (See C).

C)

**6.** Tear some strips of yellow tissue paper.

**7.** In the zigzagged center opening, glue strips of yellow tissue paper to show the flash of the exploding firecracker (See D). Glue some yellow strips to the end of the yarn. Let dry.

D)

# Chinese Symbols Banners

During the New Year celebration, Chinese families decorate their homes with the symbols for happiness, good luck, fortune, and prosperity. It is hoped that these good things will stay in the home all through the year. The symbols can be displayed by themselves or lined up together on a banner. The symbol for good luck is usually hung upside down so that good luck will pour into the home.

## What You Will Need

- tracing paper
- pencil
- white office paper
- crayons or markers
- scissors
- white glue
- red office paper
- yellow crepe-paper streamers
- clear tape
- paper clip

# WHAT TO DO

1. Use tracing paper to trace the symbols on page 42–43. Transfer the symbols onto white office paper.

2. Color the symbols with crayons or markers, or you may wish to leave them white. Cut out the symbols.

**A)**

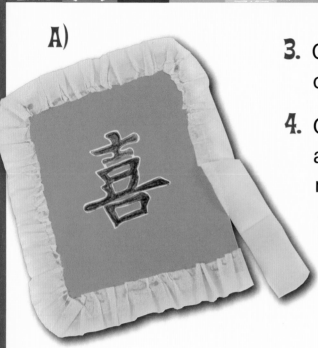

3. Glue the symbols to red office paper. Let dry.

4. Glue yellow crepe paper around the edges of the red paper (See A). Let dry.

5. Tape a paper clip to the top of the back of the red paper to use as a hanger (See B).

**B)**

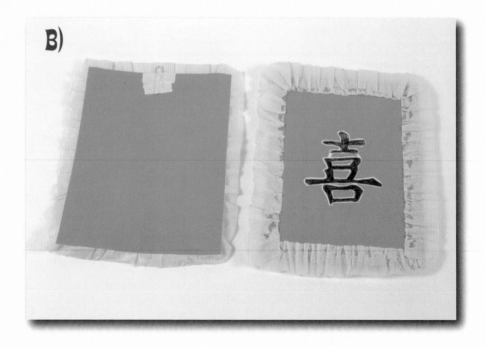

Happiness

Good Luck

Prosperity

Riches/Abundance

Here are some examples of other Chinese Symbol Banners.

# PATTERNS

Use tracing paper to copy the patterns on these pages. Ask an adult to help you cut and trace the shapes.

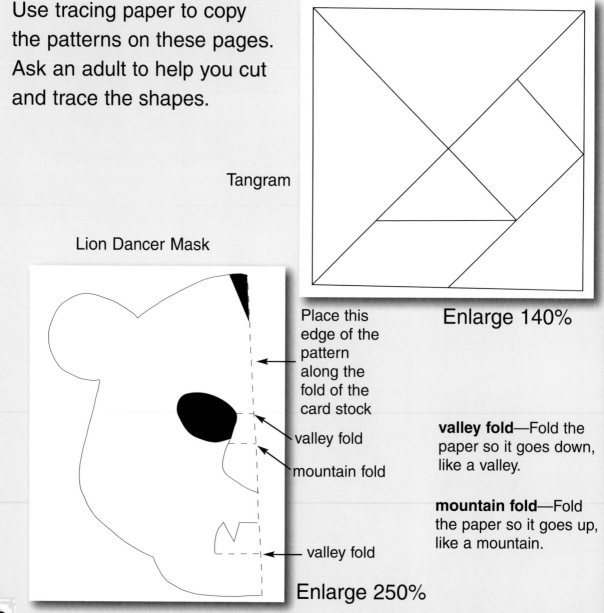

Tangram

Lion Dancer Mask

Place this edge of the pattern along the fold of the card stock

← valley fold

← mountain fold

Enlarge 140%

**valley fold**—Fold the paper so it goes down, like a valley.

**mountain fold**—Fold the paper so it goes up, like a mountain.

← valley fold

Enlarge 250%

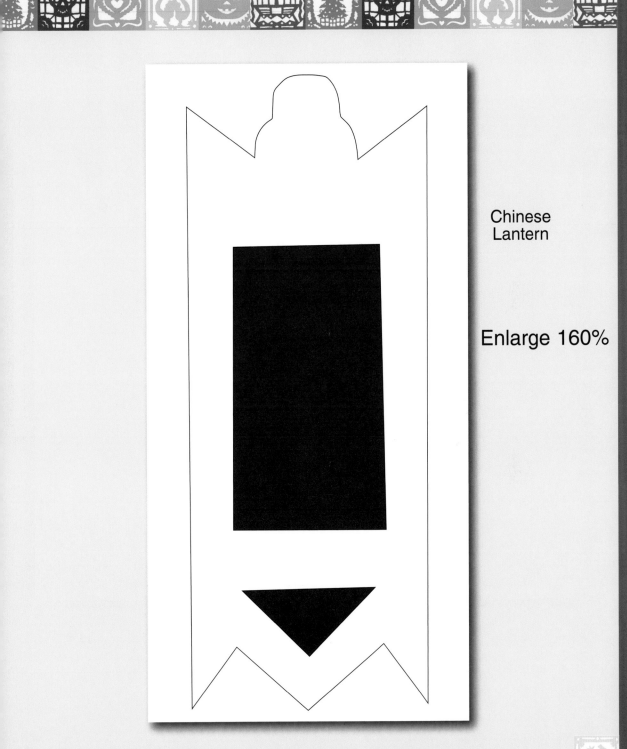

Chinese
Lantern

Enlarge 160%

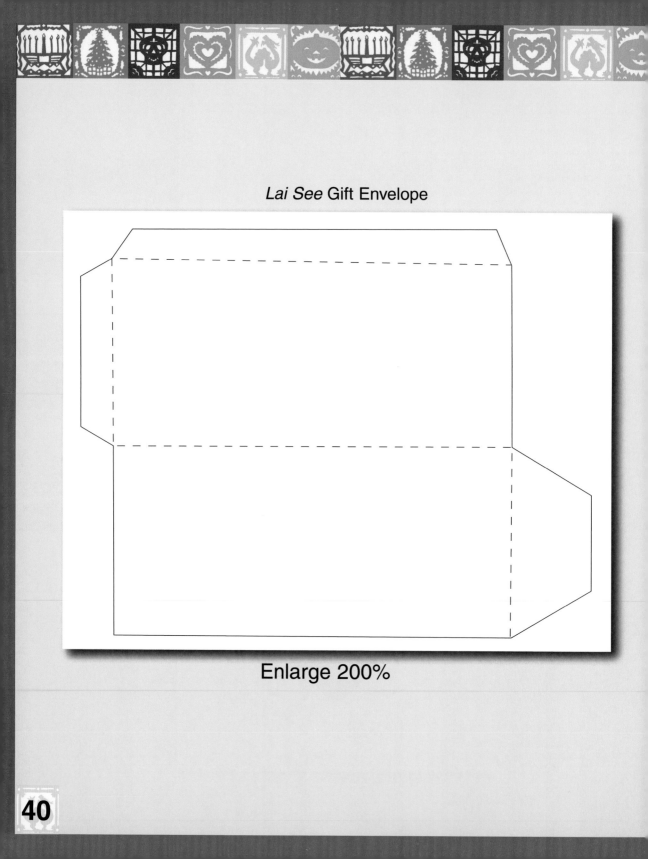

*Lai See* Gift Envelope

Enlarge 200%

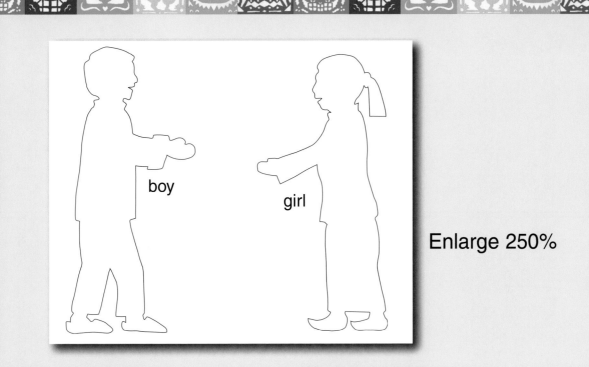

boy

girl

Enlarge 250%

Shadow Puppets

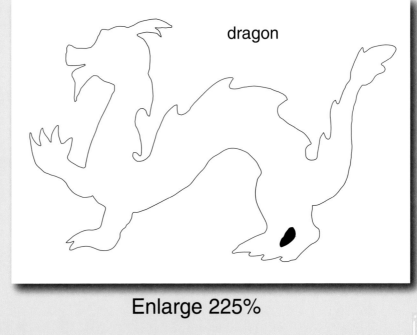

dragon

Enlarge 225%

## Chinese Symbols Banners

Good Luck

Happiness

Enlarge 150%

# Chinese Symbols Banners

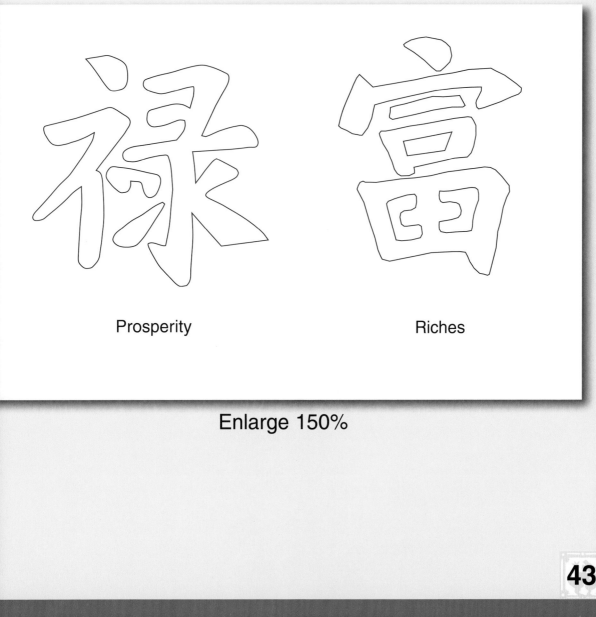

Prosperity                    Riches

## Enlarge 150%

# Read About

## Books

Casey, Dawn. *The Great Race: The Story of the Chinese Zodiac.* Cambridge, Mass.: Barefoot Books, 2006.

Jango-Cohen, Judith. *Chinese New Year.* Minneapolis, Minn.: Carolrhoda, 2005.

Olson, Kay Melchisedech. *China.* Mankato, Minn.: Blue Earth Books, 2003.

Sievert, Terri. *Chinese New Year: Festival of New Beginnings.* Mankato, Minn.: Capstone Press, 2006.

Simonds, Nina, Leslie Swartz, and the Children's Museum of Boston. *Moonbeams, Dumplings & Dragon Boats: A Treasury of Chinese Holiday Tales, Activities & Recipes.* San Diego, Calif.: Harcourt Inc., 2002.

Souter, Gillian. *Holiday Handiwork.* Milwaukee, Wisc.: Gareth Stevens, 2002.

## INTERNET ADDRESSES

**Celebrate Chinese New Year**
<http://www.kidsdomain.com/holiday/chineseny.html>

**Countdown to the New Year**
<http://pbskids.org/sagwa>
*Click on "Games." Click on "Countdown to the New Year."*

**Visit Randel McGee's Web site at**
<http://www.mcgeeproductions.com>

# INDEX

# About the Author

Randel McGee has been playing with paper and scissors for as long as he can remember. As soon as he was able to get a library card, he would go to the library and find the books that showed paper crafts, check them out, take them home, and try almost every craft in the book. He still checks out books on paper crafts at the library, but he also buys books to add to his own library and researches paper-craft sites on the Internet.

McGee says, "I begin by making copies of simple crafts or designs I see in books. Once I get the idea of how something is made, I begin to make changes to make the designs more personal. After a lot of trial and error, I find ways to do something new and different that is all my own. That's when the fun begins!"

McGee also liked singing and acting from a young age. He graduated college with a degree in children's theater and specialized in puppetry. After college, he taught himself ventriloquism and started performing at libraries and schools with a friendly dragon puppet named Groark. "Randel McGee and Groark" have toured throughout the United States and Asia, sharing their fun shows with young and old alike.

Groark is the star of two award-winning video series for elementary school students on character education: *Getting Along with Groark* and *The Six Pillars of Character.*

In the 1990s, McGee combined his love of making things with paper with his love of telling stories. He tells stories while making pictures cut from

paper to illustrate the tales he tells. The famous author Hans Christian Andersen also made cut-paper pictures when he told stories. McGee portrays Andersen in storytelling performances around the world.

Besides performing and making things, McGee, with the help of his wife, Marsha, likes showing librarians, teachers, fellow artists, and children the fun and educational experiences they can have with paper crafts, storytelling, drama, and puppetry. Randel McGee has belonged to the Guild of American Papercutters, the National Storytelling Network, and the International Ventriloquists' Association. He has been a regional director for the Puppeteers of America, Inc., and past president of UNIMA-USA, an international puppetry organization. He has been active in working with children and scouts in his community and church for many years. He and his wife live in California. They are the parents of five grown children who are all talented artists and performers.